The Bibliot

Charles Nodier

Alpha Editions

This edition published in 2024

ISBN : 9789367241677

Design and Setting By
Alpha Editions
www.alphaedis.com
Email - info@alphaedis.com

As per information held with us this book is in Public Domain.
This book is a reproduction of an important historical work. Alpha Editions uses the best technology to reproduce historical work in the same manner it was first published to preserve its original nature. Any marks or number seen are left intentionally to preserve its true form.

Contents

PREFACE .... - 1 -

THE BIBLIOMANIAC .... - 7 -

THE BIBLIOMANIAC .... - 8 -

NOTES .... - 29 -

PREFACE

"GOOD, AMIABLE NODIER," are the words by which the world, apart from scholars, characterizes Charles Nodier. He is portrayed with a flowered vest, and a frock-coat with great lapels, finished by one of those collars which, by an easy play upon words, are called *les cols (l'école) des vieillards*. Nodier's collar, which turned up slightly at the points in a Prudhommesque manner, touched the corners of his refined, kindly mouth; but it is difficult immediately to associate the remembrance of certain books with this 1835 face, for time obliterates everything.

If Nodier belonged by right of his first literary impressions to the classical school, his liberal spirit soon identified itself with that of the romanticists. His face, full of genial originality, bore the characteristics of a man living between two literary epochs; but history little by little soon effaced all these tints and shades. Nodier was also one of those improvisators who talked their books. Contemporaries, in reading them, seemed to hear him speak, and a little imagination added to the surprises of these written conversations; but when the voice ceases the charm vanishes.

It is certain that the reader of to-day is somewhat at a loss in the company of a book of Nodier's, and feels very much as when, in a military panorama, he sees the wheel of a real caisson, and often a veritable cannon and cannon-ball, which at first sight blend with the painted canvas, until it is difficult to say where the actual ends and the illusion begins. If we read his reminiscences and studies of his own time in a credulous spirit, we shall constantly say, "Nodier is mistaken; what he tells us is not only wholly improbable but impossible, and is completely at variance with history"— until the wise reader decides that Nodier's entire writings should bear the title of one of his books, "Contes et Fantaisies."

Perhaps it would be interesting to separate the true from the false in these works of Nodier, and to show how the thread of truth disappears under his embroidery. In confining the investigation to this little book, "The Bibliomaniac," taken from "Les Contes de la Veillée,"[1] and rejuvenated by the illustrations of Maurice Leloir, one may have the pleasure of bringing to light, by the aid of letters and comparisons, the best and most absorbing passion that controlled Nodier. Is it not a summary of his passion, from the first lines? If he left the Arsenal Library, where he had been appointed librarian at the end of the year 1823 by a bibliographical minister, M. de Corbière, it was to stroll among the old book-dealers. If he wrote to the friend of his childhood, who became his lifelong confidant, his fellow-countryman of Franche-Comté, Charles Weiss, it was a litany of bibliographical enthusiasm. Small as his means were, Nodier had the incurable mania of book-buying. The noun and the adjective are his own words. But, he said one day, this craze is no more vain in its final results than any other of the illusions of life. Also, in perusing the sayings of the hero of this story, Theodore, we feel that Nodier sympathizes with him from the bottom of his heart. Theodore sometimes resembles him like a brother, and we cannot help regretting that Nodier could not wholly make up his mind to amuse himself fully at his own expense, or to take from real life a man he knew very well, rather than treat him incidentally.

This original and true bibliomaniac, for Nodier's Theodore is merely a degenerate bibliophile, was celebrated at the time of the Restoration. He was a lawyer named Boulard, who, instead of admiring an imposing row of books in his cabinet, like his fellows, only took pleasure in arranging them on the shelves, or in piling them up in his closets. His library was scattered everywhere in this strange study, which overflowed with cheap literature from auction sales. Finally, there was such an invasion of books that Boulard, becoming the owner of the house in which he lived, expelled all his tenants in turn, and took possession himself of floor after floor for the storage of his books. After this he bought six other houses which he turned into depositories for books. One day, when Nodier asked him for a certain book, Boulard, going from one house to another, struck the stacks, the walls, the ramparts, of books with his cane, saying in triumphant irony, "It is either here or there." Boulard, growing ill, and no longer able to go out, had the books brought to his bed. He handled them, asked their price, and held them up with admiring affection. As his memory became more and more impaired, he would buy the same book three or four times over. His family, worried at his growing mania, and not desiring to oppose the fervor of his wishes, which were turning violently to certain fixed ideas, conceived the plan of showing him a great part of his own books, which he no longer recognized, as if they were new acquisitions. This gave him a joyous surprise at every moment, and Boulard, having thus delightfully reviewed all his past life, went to sleep forever, over a book, in 1825.

The remembrance of his death doubtless inspired Nodier with the half-sad, half-amusing ending of his Bibliomaniac. Boulard was the type of bibliomaniac whose progressive malady would be the most interesting to study. What was Nodier's object, then, in searching here and there for materials with which to sketch an imaginary figure, when the notary was at hand? Nodier always followed the plan of taking his imagination as a guide; but imagination has also its moods and caprices, and it is a mistake for an author to be so fanciful that he ceases to follow the simple and fertile lead of nature.

Nodier could have chosen still another original, the Dutch baron Westreeven van Tiellandt. This extraordinary person kept his library under triple lock for forty years. One day, however, in an access of good feeling, he said to two of his best friends: "You have often expressed a desire to see my books. I want to oblige you both, but you must submit to certain conditions: before entering my library you must each put on a dressing-gown which I have expressly prepared, because your clothes might be saturated with a smell which is bad for books; and you must wear the slippers that I have provided, because your shoes might be full of dangerous dust." The baron, however, invariably found an excuse for postponing the visit to his library, and died without having kept his promise. As the baron survived Nodier some years, this last feature could not have been portrayed with its attendant moral. The "Bulletin du Bibliophile," which owed its existence in part to Nodier, took upon itself the baron's funeral oration and reproduced his will. In leaving his library to the city of The Hague, the baron stipulated that it should be open only on the first and third Thursdays of each month, and only to people who had been provided the preceding day with cards of admission. "Never," he said, "under any pretext, shall the books or manuscripts be taken outside the reading-room." No further purchases were to be made, except to complete the collections which he had himself begun—he whose restless and jealous spirit wished to hover around his books.

Avarice, either in the Latin sense of the word or in its more modern meaning, is the agony of a man who is made to tremble by every trifle when he contemplates his possessions. Some of these bibliomaniacs are like very rich people, of whom it is said, "They leave a great fortune." The verb "to leave" has here rather an ironical meaning. It is as much as saying that they have amassed wealth without having been themselves the gainers thereby.

The book-collector belongs to a race of refined egotists. He knows and tastes the subtle, intense joy which comes from the sight and possession of a fine book. Even before opening it, he handles it caressingly, touching its pages lightly as he would the wings of a butterfly.

In order not to stray too far from the pictures of other days which Nodier evoked, let us look at the charming type of a book-collector who was worthy of the name: Silvestre de Sacy. During the eighteen years of the reign of Louis Philippe, Sacy might have been seen lounging along the quays, on his way to the Palais Bourbon, where he followed the parliamentary debates in his journalistic vocation, carrying almost always a selection of Madame de Sévigné's letters in his hand. When he returned home it was to take Montaigne, Bossuet, or some other classic, clothed in bindings worthy of them, from a shelf close at hand. By this daily reading he added to his mixture of Christianity and philosophy; but as he cared only for the best editions, he was afraid of rich men, and regarded them as the absorbers of fine books. *Multi vocati, pauci lecti*,—many are called, but few read,—was what D'Argenson had already proposed as an inscription for the library of a *fermier général*.[2] Sacy, when he dreamed, on the eve of a book sale, of this or that volume which he coveted, and which he feared he might not be able to hold successfully against the fancy or caprice of some financier, would have palpitation of the heart. Prévost-Paradol wrote of him: "This Christian, whom some would like to call austere, if the word austerity could cover so much forbearance and perfect gentleness, became a sort of epicure in all that concerned his reading."

The love of books was such a part of his life that when some one asked for his autograph, to add to one of his lithographic portraits,—a picture in which he lives again, peaceful, mischievous, and benevolent, all at the same time, like a citizen of the true, liberal, and literary race,—he could not refrain from declaring, in a half page which is reproduced in facsimile, that of all passions that of the book-collector is ever the best. Even though his eyes suffered severely from fatigue, it did not discourage his ardent affection for his books. Has he not said in one of those confidences in which lies the charm of his criticisms, "If I become blind I think I shall still take pleasure in holding a beautiful book in my hand. I shall at least feel the softness of its binding, and imagine that I can see it: I have seen so many!"

"O my beloved books," he wrote in connection with the dispersion of a library, "some day you will also be exhibited in an auction-room, when you will pass into other hands, owners perhaps less worthy of you than your present master. Yet these books that I have selected, one by one, are truly mine, collected by the sweat of my brow; and I love them so, that it seems to me they have become a part of my very soul by such a long and precious intercourse."

There speaks the bibliophile, who loves books as they ought to be loved, who lives with them, asks their advice, and cherishes and protects them against their numerous enemies. An English typographer[3] thus enumerates the enemies of books: "Fire, water, gas, heat, dust, neglect, ignorance, rats, mice, and finally bookbinders,"—adding the last with the sudden anger of a man who has suffered by having some fine book hopelessly cut down. He might have mentioned an enemy still more dangerous, the most difficult of all to vanquish—an enemy of every day and hour, ever present, and ready alike for open warfare or for subterfuge: woman.

With a few rare and conspicuous exceptions, women are anti-bibliophiles or book-haters. A book in their eyes is merely a newspaper: they crease and crumple it as they turn its leaves. Lacking a paper-knife to cut the edges, they use a card, a pin, or even a hair-pin. If a rare book is under discussion, they appear more interested in the smallest trifle than in all the first editions that exist. They prefer a scrap of ribbon to the most exquisite binding. If you take from its shrine a miniature volume, unique enough to make a book-lover turn pale with delight, do not trust it to a woman, for in opening it she will split its back. The best of husbands may give the key of his safe to his wife, but he must not give her, even for one moment, the key of his library. A woman should never be left alone with a book, and such in fact should be the rule with all married book-lovers.

Nodier said that, after woman, books are the most delightful things in the world. Why do not women comprehend this, and increase their influence by their appreciation of books?

Following the bibliomaniac who hoards, and the bibliophile who collects, according to the very correct terms of Nodier, come the amateurs of the old book-cult. Nodier and Sacy give them the incorrect title of *bouquiniste* (dealer in old books), when their knowledge as Academicians should have made them use the word *bouquineur* (old-book hunter) in order to avoid confusion. To their ears *bouquiniste* evidently had a pleasing sound. How Sacy despised the collector of dirty, damaged books, which were fit only to be sent to a book-hospital, supposing such a place to exist!

"I know him!" cried Sacy in a rage,—"this amateur who buys books for three or five cents, or in a moment of folly even paying as much as six cents. In other things he is a man of wit and taste, a polite man and a good companion, whose only depravity is concerning books."

If you have the curiosity to learn the identity of this charming man with the single unpardonable fault, it can be found in a little book of memoirs by Étienne Delécluze, an editor of the "Journal des Débats." He says that nothing was more amusing than the quarrels which arose between Sacy and Saint-Marc Girardin on the subject of books—the one being unable to find either text or binding of sufficient beauty to express the admiration inspired by the writings of Cicero and Molière, Fénelon and Montaigne; the other careless about the exterior condition of a book, but eager to know its contents. These two charming minds have created laughter more than once when, in answer to the tantalizing tone in which Saint-Marc uttered the word *bibliophile* (collector of best editions), Sacy would reply with humorous gaiety, "You are only a *bouquiniste*" (old-book dealer).

While these figures float and vanish, between the lines of the bibliomaniac appears the figure of a philosophic *bouquineur*, who comes closer to us, and who has often been seen by the frequenters of the quays. It is Xavier Marmier. He walked from box to box with short steps, his only journeys then being among the trays of the book-dealers—this man who in former times had been such a great traveller. A little broken by his eighty years, and his lower lip drooping, his expression at the same time was kindly and intelligent, bearing the marks both of easy skepticism and extreme good will. He would turn the books over, ask the price, and slip two or three volumes into the deep pockets of his blue coat.

One day he said to me, with an air of triumph, "I have just bought the first edition of one of my own books. This fact of its being the first edition, however, does not add much to the value of the book; but these 'Lettres sur le Nord' have shivered so long in the box, and have spent so many weeks in the same place, that I took pity on them."

Then Marmier told me with provincial gaiety that the seller—a gamin who, strangely enough, did not know him—had asked him two francs for the copy.

"Two francs!" exclaimed Marmier.

"Yes, sir; that is what it is worth. It is by Marmier."

"Hum! hum! I know that it is by Marmier, but that does not make it worth two francs."

"But, sir, he is an Academician."

"]Are you sure of that?"

"Yes, sir; it says so on the cover."

"But has he not been dead a long time?"

"That I do not know, but it is possible that he has."

"See here," said Marmier, "dead or alive he is not worth more than thirty sous."

"Well, then, you may have it."

And Marmier, very happy, took the book, intending to give it to some old friend, "who perhaps will not sell it before to-morrow," he said.

Dear, good man, who from searching in many boxes had found true wisdom—not to be deceived, and to be lenient. "Ah! book-hunting is the best passion that I can wish you," he said, the last time that I saw him, when he was weak, and walked with difficulty, but looked calmly into the face of death.

Bouquinistes, bibliophiles, and bibliomaniacs all live happily because of this passion, and bless it. Charles Nodier knew its delightful anxieties so well that, a few hours before he died, his last thought—so his daughter

Madame Mennessier-Nodier writes, in the book that she has affectionately consecrated to him—was to dictate an account of a few trifling debts that he owed his binders and the booksellers.

R. V<small>ALLERY</small>-R<small>ADOT</small>.

THE BIBLIOMANIAC

THE BIBLIOMANIAC

YOU all know Theodore. I have come to strew some flowers upon his grave, praying heaven that the earth may touch him lightly.

These two familiar phrases will tell you plainly that I am about to consecrate some pages to him as an obituary notice or funeral oration.

It is twenty years since Theodore retired from the world, to work or to be idle: which of the two was a great secret. He dreamed, and no one knew what he dreamed about. He passed his life surrounded by books, and occupied himself with nothing else, which gave some people the idea that he was writing a book which would supersede all other books; but they were evidently mistaken.

Theodore had studied too much not to know that this book had been written three hundred years ago. It was the thirteenth chapter of the first book of Rabelais.

Theodore no longer talked, nor laughed, neither played cards or gambled, nor ate, no longer went to balls or to the theatre. The women whom he had loved in his youth no longer attracted him, or at most he looked only at their feet; and when some elegant and brilliantly colored footgear caught his attention, alas! he would say, heaving a sigh from the depths of his chest, there is a great waste of good morocco! He had formerly followed the fashions. Those who remember the time, tell us that he was the first to tie his cravat on the left side, notwithstanding the dictum of Garat, who tied his on the right, and in spite of the common herd, who still continue to tie theirs in the middle.

Theodore was no longer worried by the fashions. He had only one dispute with his tailor during twenty years: "Sir," he said to him one day, "it will be the last coat I shall take from you, if you again forget to make my pockets in quarto."

Politics, by whose vagaries so many fools have made their fortunes, had never tempted him from his reveries for more than a moment. Politics put him in a bad temper. After Napoleon's futile enterprise in the North, which raised the price of russia leather, he welcomed the French intervention in the Spanish revolution. "This," he said, "is a good chance to bring chivalric romances and the *Cancioneros* from the Peninsula." But the expeditionary army did not think of it, and he was vexed. When any one said *Trocadero* to him, he would reply ironically, *Romancero*, which made him pass for a Liberal.

M. de Bourmont's campaign on the African coast transported him with joy. "Thank heaven!" he said, rubbing his hands; "we shall have cheap levant morocco." This made him pass for a Carlist.

He was walking one summer's day in a crowded street, collating a book, when some men, who were coming with a staggering gait from a saloon, commanded him, knife at throat, to cry in the name

of liberty, "Long live the Poles!" "I ask nothing better," said Theodore, whose perpetual thought was an eternal cry in favor of the human race; "but may I ask why?" "Because we declare war against Holland, who oppresses Poland under the pretext that they do not like the Jesuits," replied the friend of light, who was a rude geographer and a fearless logician. "God forgive us!" muttered our friend, crossing his hands

- 10 -

piteously. "Shall we not in this case be obliged to use M. Montgolfier's imitation Holland paper?"

The product of modern civilization answered by breaking Theodore's leg with a blow of his stick.

Theodore stayed in his bed for three months, examining book-catalogues. Always disposed to carry his feelings to extremes, this reading fevered his blood.

Even in his convalescence his sleep was horribly uneasy. One night his wife roused him from the tortures of the nightmare. "You came just in time," he said, embracing her, "to save me from dying of grief and fear. I was surrounded by monsters who would give me no quarter."

"What monsters do you dread, my dear?" she said,—"you who have never injured any one."

"It was, if I remember rightly, the ghost of Purgold whose fatal shears devoured an inch and a half of the margins of my uncut Aldus, while the shade of Heudier pitilessly plunged my most beautiful *editio princeps* into a devouring acid, withdrawing it entirely bleached; but I have good reason to think that they are at least both in purgatory."

    His wife thought that he was talking Greek, because he knew a little Greek, and as a proof of his knowledge three shelves in his library were filled with Greek books with uncut leaves. He never opened them either, but was satisfied to show them by the side or back to his most intimate acquaintances, telling with calm assurance the place where they were printed, the date, and the printer's name. The simple-minded considered him a sorcerer. But about this there is a difference of opinion.

As he was wasting away under their very eyes, his family called in a physician, who was both a philosopher and a man of intelligence.

You will discover if this was the case. This physician saw that congestion of the brain was imminent, and made an elaborate report of this disease in the "Journal des Sciences Médicales," where it figures under the name of morocco monomania or bibliomaniac's typhus; but it was not a question for the Academy of Sciences, because the illness was in conjunction with cholera morbus.

They advised him to take exercise; and, as the idea amused him, we started out early one day, for I could not trust him to go a step alone. We turned toward the quays, and I was rejoicing because I thought that the sight of the river would revive him; but he never took his eyes from the level of the parapets. They were as free from show-cases as if they had been visited early in the morning by the public censor, who in February had sent the archiepiscopal library in swimming.[4] We were more fortunate at the Quai aux Fleurs, where books were in profusion. But what books! All the works which the newspapers had puffed during the last month, and which had gone from the

publisher's office, or the bookseller, into the ten-cent box. Authors of every kind and sort, philosophers, historians, poets, novelists, who could not be wafted to immortality by the most alluring advertisements, and whose works go unheeded from the shelves of the store to the banks of the Seine, a deep Lethe, where they contemplate, while decaying, the certain end of their presumptive flight. I turned over there the pages of some of my octavos, which were placed between those of five or six of my friends.

Theodore sighed, but it was not because he saw the works of my brain exposed to the rain, owing to the scanty protection of an oil-cloth cover.

"What has become of the golden age of the outdoor venders of old books? It was here, certainly, that my famous friend Barbier collected his treasures until he was able to make a precise bibliography of several thousand items. It was here that Monmerqué, on his way to the Palais, and wise Laboudrie, while leaving the city, walked for hours with instruction and profit. It was from here that old Boulard carried away daily a yard of rarities, measuring them with his surveyor's cane,—volumes for which there was no place reserved in his six houses stuffed with books. How often on such occasions had he desired the modest *angulus*[5] of Horace, or the elastic cover of the fairies' tent, which if necessary could shield the whole army of Xerxes, and which might be carried as easily in one's belt as the knife-sheath of Jeannot's grandfather. Now, more's the pity, you see only fragments of modern literature which will never become ancient, whose life will have evaporated in twenty-four hours, like that of the flies of the river Hypanis: a literature worthy in truth of the charcoal ink and pulp paper used by mercenary printers, who are almost as foolish as the books. It is profaning the name of books to give it to these black-blotted rags, whose destinies have not even changed in leaving the basket on the rag-picker's shoulders. The quays henceforth are the morgue for contemporary celebrities."

He sighed again, and I sighed too, but it was for a different reason.

I was in a hurry to lead him away, because his increasing excitement seemed to threaten him at any moment with a fatal attack. It must have been an unlucky day, for everything combined to increase his melancholy.

"See," he said, in passing the showy shop-front of Ladvocat, "the *Galliot du Pré*[6] of the debased literature of the nineteenth century; a liberal, industrious bookseller, who deserved to have been born in a better time, but whose deplorable activity has cruelly multiplied new books, to the everlasting injury of the old; an unpardonable patron of cotton-made paper, of incorrect spelling, and of stilted illustrations; a fatal protector of academic prose and fashionable poetry: as if France had produced any poetry since Ronsard, or any prose after Montaigne! This bookseller's palace is like the Trojan horse that held the thieves of the Palladium—like Pandora's box, which let loose all the evils of the earth. But yet I like this cannibal, and I shall be a chapter in his book, but I shall not see him again!"

"Look," he continued, "there is Crozet's store with the green walls. He is the most agreeable of our young booksellers, the man of all Paris who can best distinguish between a binding by Derome the elder and Derome the younger, and the last hope of a passing generation of amateurs, if the cult of old books should return in the midst of our barbarity. But I shall not enjoy his conversation to-day, even though I always learn something from it. He is in England, where he is competing, by the right of retaliation, with the greedy usurers of Soho Square and Fleet Street for the precious fragments of the monuments of our beautiful language which have been forgotten for two centuries on the ungrateful soil that produced them. *Macte animo, generoso puer!...*"

"Here," he said, retracing his steps,—"here is the Pont-des-Arts, with its useless side-rails only a few centimeters wide, affording no support for the noble folios of three centuries, majestic volumes with pigskin covers and bronze clasps, which have delighted the eyes of ten generations. This is truly an emblematic bridge, leading from the Palais to the Institute by a path which is not the path of science. I do not know whether I am mistaken, but the invention of a bridge of this kind should be a startling illustration to the erudite of the decadence of good literature."

"There," said Theodore, passing the white sign of an active and ingenious bookseller in the Place du Louvre, "that sign has made my heart palpitate for a long time; but I no longer see it without a sensation of pain, since Techener has reprinted with Tastu's characters, on showy paper, and under an enticing cover, the gothic marvels of Jehan Bonfons of Paris, Jehan Mareschal of Lyons, and Jehan de Chaney of Avignon, unobtainable trifles until he produced them in delightful facsimile. Snow-white paper fills me with horror, my friend; and there is nothing that I like less, except this same paper when it has received from the stroke of a cruel pressman, the deplorable imprint of the visions and idiocies of this iron age."

Theodore sighed more frequently, and was rapidly growing worse.

We thus came in the Rue des Bons-Enfants, to the literary bazaar where Silvestre held his auction sales. It was a place honored by learned men, which has seen more priceless curios during a quarter of a century than the library of the Ptolemies ever held (which library perhaps was not burned by Omar, whatever our twaddling historians may say). I had never seen so many splendid books on exhibition.

"Unfortunate people who have to sell them," I said to Theodore.

"They are dead," he said, "or it would kill them."

But the hall was empty. No one was to be seen except the indefatigable M. Thour, who was patiently cataloguing upon cards the titles of the books which had escaped his notice the previous day. The happiest among all men is he who has at his command, and accurately arranged, a faithful transcription of the title-pages of all known books. It is nothing to him if all the productions of printing are destroyed in the next revolution which the perfection of progress promises us. He can leave to posterity the complete catalogue of the universal library. He would have admirable forethought in seeing from afar the necessity for compiling this inventory of civilization. A few years more, and civilization will be no longer spoken about.

"God forgive me, Theodore," said Silvestre; "you have mistaken the day. Those books that you see were sold yesterday in the last session, and are waiting for the porter to deliver them." Theodore reeled and turned pale. His face assumed the tint of old citron morocco. I felt the blow that had struck him, to the bottom of my own heart.

"It is no matter," he said, with an altered manner. "I recognize only my usual ill luck in this bad news. But to whom do these things belong, these pearls and diamonds, these wonderful riches in which the libraries of de Thou and Grolier would have gloried?"

"As usual, sir," Silvestre answered, "these original editions of the classics, these perfect old copies with the autographs of celebrated scholars, these piquant philological curiosities, of which academy and university have never heard, rightfully revert to Richard Heber.[7] It is the British lion's share, to whom we are willing to surrender, with good grace, the Greek and Latin classics which we have ceased to understand. These fine collections of natural history, these masterpieces of workmanship and pictorial art, belong to Prince ———, who uses his studious tastes to still further enhance his great fortune. These mysteries of the middle ages, these phœnix-like precepts whose counterpart[8] is no longer in existence, these curious dramatic attempts of our ancestors, will swell the model library of M. de Soleine. These well-preserved facetiæ, so strikingly subtle and enjoyable, have been purchased by your friend M. Aimé-Martin. I need not tell you to whom these fresh, brilliant morocco bindings belong, with the triple fillets, wide dentelle, and sumptuous panels. He is the Shakespeare among the minor collectors, the Corneille of melodrama, the graceful and often eloquent interpreter of the feelings and virtues of the populace, who, after having depreciated the value of books in the morning, bought them for their weight in gold in the evening, not, however, without grinding his teeth like a mortally wounded boar, and turning a tragic eye, veiled by black eyebrows, upon his rivals."

Theodore had ceased to listen. He was handling a beautiful volume that he

hurriedly measured with his Elzevirometer, a six-inch measure divided almost to infinity, by which he regulated the price, and, alas! the intrinsic merit also, of his books. He measured the accursed book ten times and as many times verified the troublesome calculation, muttered some words that I did not understand, finally changed color, and fainted in my arms. I had great difficulty in getting him into a passing carriage.

For a long time my attempts to learn the cause of his sudden grief were futile. He did not speak. He did not hear my words. It is the typhus fever, I thought, and the crisis of the fever.

I held him in my arms. I continued to question him. At last he spoke.

"You see in me," he said, "the most unhappy of men. That book is the 1676 Virgil, on large paper, of which I thought that I had the best example known, and yet this is taller than mine, by the third of a line.[9] Prejudiced or spiteful minds might even call it half a line. A third of a line, good God!"

I was confounded. I saw that the delirium was increasing.

"A third of a line," he repeated, shaking his fist furiously in the air like Ajax or Capaneus. All my limbs trembled.

He gradually fell into a state of deep depression.

The poor man lived only to suffer. He repeated from time to time, "The third of a line!" and wrung his hands, while I kept saying, in an undertone, "Confusion to books and typhus fever!"

"Calm yourself, my friend," I whispered gently in his ear, each time the paroxysm was renewed. "A third of a line is not much, even in the most particular things of life."

"Not much?" he cried; "a third of a line in the 1676 Virgil! It was the third of a line that raised the price of the Nerli Homer at M. de Cotte's[10] a hundred louis. A third of a line! Ah! would you count the third of a line nothing in the length of a dagger that pierced your heart?"

His expression again wholly changed, his arms became rigid, his legs were seized with cramps as in a vise. The typhus was visibly reaching the extremities. I did not desire to lengthen by even the third of a line the short distance that separated us from the house.

At last we arrived there.

"A third of a line," he said to the concierge.

"A third of a line," he said to the cook, who opened the door.

"A third of a line," he said to his wife, with a flood of tears.

"My parrot has flown away!" cried his little girl, likewise weeping.

"Why did you leave the cage open?" replied Theodore. "A third of a line!"

"There is an uprising in the South and in the Rue du Cadran," said the old aunt, who was reading the evening paper.

"What the devil are the people meddling with?" answered Theodore. "A third of a line!"

"Your farm at la Beauce has been burned," said his servant in putting him to bed.

"It must be rebuilt," said Theodore, "if it is worth the trouble. A third of a line!"

"Do you think that this is serious?" the nurse asked me.

"Your question proves, my good woman, that you have not read the 'Journal des Sciences Médicales.' Why do you delay in getting a priest?"

Happily at that minute the curé came in to converse, as was his custom, about the thousand and one literary and bibliographical trifles from which his breviary had not wholly distracted him; but he forgot them all when he felt Theodore's pulse.

"Alas! my child," he said, "the life of man is only a journey, and even the world itself is not set upon everlasting foundations. It must end like everything that has a beginning."

"Have you read, on this subject," said Theodore, "the 'Treatise on the World, its Origin and its Antiquity'?"

"I learned all that I know from the book of Genesis," said the conservative pastor; "but I have heard it said that M. de Mirabeau, a sophist of the last century, had written a book upon this subject."

"*Sub judice lis est*," Theodore interrupted brusquely. "I have proved in my 'Stromates' that the first two parts of 'Le Monde' were by that dreadfully pedantic Mirabeau, and the third was by the Abbé Lemascrier."

"Ah! my goodness," said the old aunt, taking off her spectacles; "then who was it that made America?"

"This is not the question now," continued the abbé. "Do you believe in the Trinity?"

"How could I disbelieve the famous volume of Servetus, 'De Trinitate,'" said Theodore, half raising himself on his pillow, "when I have seen an example go, *ipsissimis oculis*, for the trifling sum of two hundred and fifteen francs at the MacCarthy sale, while at the dispersal of the La Vallière collection it brought seven hundred?"[11]

"We are straying from the point," exclaimed the priest, a little disconcerted. "I wish to know, my son, what you think of the divinity of Jesus Christ."

"Well!" said Theodore, "it depends upon what you mean by it. I shall maintain against every one that the 'Toldos-Jeschu,' which was written by that ignorant railler Voltaire, who wasted on it a lot of foolish fables worthy of the 'Thousand and One Nights,' is nothing but evil rabbinesque nonsense, unworthy to be placed in the library of a scholar."

"That is well!" sighed the worthy ecclesiastic.

"At least," Theodore continued, "unless some one should discover the large-paper copy, of which there is a hint, if my memory serves me, in the bibliographic jumble of David Clement."[12]

The curé groaned audibly, and, rising from his chair, bent over Theodore to make him clearly understand, without ambiguity or equivocation, that he was in the last stage of the bibliomaniac's typhus which is spoken of in the "Journal des Sciences Médicales," and that he should not think of anything but his salvation.

Theodore had never intrenched himself behind that insolent negation of unbelievers which is the science of fools; but the dear man had pushed the useless study of the letter, in books, too far to comprehend the spirit. In a perfect state of health a doctrine of any kind would give him a fever, or a dogma induce lockjaw. In a theological matter he would have lowered his colors before a Saint-Simonian. He turned his face to the wall.

A long time passed without a word, and we should have thought that he was dead, except as I bent close to him I heard him murmur feebly, "A third of a line! God of goodness and justice! but where will you give me back that third of a line, and how far can your omnipotence retrieve the irreparable error of that binder?"

One of his friends, a bibliophile, came in a minute later. They told him that Theodore was in the last agony; that he was delirious to the point of thinking that the Abbé Lemascrier had made the third part of the world; and that he had lost his power of speech a quarter of an hour before.

"I am going to make sure of it," said the amateur. "By what mistake in pagination do we recognize the genuine 1635 Elzevir edition of Cæsar?" he asked Theodore.

"153 for 149."

"Very good. And of the Terence of the same year?"

"108 for 104."

"The devil!" I said; "the Elzevirs played in bad luck with their figures that year. They were wise not to choose it for the printing of their logarithms."

"Wonderful!" continued Theodore's friend. "If I had listened to these people here, I should have believed that you were at the point of death."

"A third of a line," replied Theodore, whose voice was failing by degrees.

"I know your story, but it is nothing in comparison with mine. Think what I lost, eight days ago, in one of those bastard, nameless sales which are advertised only by a placard on the door,—a Boccaccio of 1527,[13] as beautiful as your own, the binding of Venetian vellum, with the pointed a's proved throughout, and not a leaf repaired."

All Theodore's faculties concentrated in one idea.

"Are you very sure that the a's were pointed?"

"As pointed as the iron tip of a lancer's halberd."

"It was then, doubtless, the 'Vintisettine' itself."

"Its very self. We had a jolly dinner that day: charming women, fresh oysters, intelligent people, and champagne. I reached the sale three minutes after the hammer fell."

"Sir," cried Theodore in a fury, "when the 'Vintisettine' is to be sold, one does not dine!"

His vitality, which had been sustained by the excitement of the conversation, as the bellows revives a dying spark, was exhausted by his last effort. His lips muttered once more, "A third of a line!" but they were his last words.

At the time that we gave up all hope of his recovery, we moved his bed near to his book-shelves, from which we took down, one by one, every book for which he seemed to ask with his eyes, letting him look the longest at those that we thought would please him the most.

He died at midnight, lying between a Du Seuil and a Padeloup, his hands lovingly clasping a Thouvenin.

The next day we followed his hearse, at the head of a great crowd of sorrowful morocco-finishers, and we sealed his tomb with a stone bearing the following inscription, which he had parodied for himself from Franklin's epitaph:

HERE LIES, IN
ITS WOODEN BINDING,
A FOLIO COPY OF THE BEST
EDITION OF MAN, WRITTEN IN
THE LANGUAGE OF A GOLDEN
AGE, WHICH THE WORLD
NO LONGER UNDERSTANDS.
TO-DAY
IT IS A SPOILED
OLD BOOK,
STAINED AND
IMPERFECT, LACKING THE TITLE-PAGE,
WORM-EATEN AND INJURED
BY DECAY. WE
DARE NOT ANTICIPATE
FOR IT THE USELESS
HONOR OF A
REPRINT.

NOTES

[1] In the bibliography of Nodier's writings, published with the catalogue of his library, Paris, 1844, the first edition of "Le Bibliomane" is registered 1832-1833, as in tome I of "Livre des Cent et un."

[2] Fermier général. An association existed in France, from the reign of Philip the Fair until the Revolution of 1789, possessing the right, by purchase, to levy taxes on various articles of consumption. These "farmers" were mostly uneducated parvenus, and their extortions were so great that though they paid no less than one hundred and eighty millions of francs for the monopoly the last year of its existence, immense fortunes were made by all concerned. The Revolution caused the abolition of the privilege, and all the "farmers" were executed.

[3] "The Enemies of Books," by William Blades.

[4] During the riots of February, 1831, a mob of self-elected "public censors" attacked the palace of the Archbishop of Paris at Notre Dame, destroyed many valuable paintings, ruined the furniture, and threw a large part of the library into the Seine.

[5] ANGULUS. A secret nook or corner, meaning, in this instance, the Sabine farm presented to Horace by Mæcenas, which the poet declared in his "Odes" to be all-sufficient for his needs.

[6] Galliot du Pré flourished in Paris during the middle of the sixteenth century. His publications, for the most part, bear the device of a galley propelled by sails and oars, with the legend "Vogue la Gualee."

[7] The library of Richard Heber was sold a few years after this supposed incident. The various sessions of the auction occupied portions of two hundred days, from 1834 to 1836.

[8] Nodier used the term "ménecheme," or twin brother, a word taken from a comedy by Plautus.

[9] The thirty-sixth part of an inch.

[10] "HOMERI OPERA, græce. Florentiæ, sumptibus Bern. et Nerii Nerliorum. 1488." Two volumes, folio. The first edition of Homer, printed at the expense of the brothers Nerli, after a copy prepared by Demetrius Chalcondyles of Athens. The De Cotte copy was uncut, and sold for 3601 francs. It was bought by M. Caillard, and passed into the Bibliothèque du Roi after his death, where it replaced a vellum copy that the French were constrained to return to the library of Saint Marc, Venice.

[11] The "Trinitate" of Servetus: a small octavo, printed in 1531. A copy was sold as indicated. See Brunet's "Manuel du Libraire."

[12] "BIBLIOTHÈQUE CURIEUSE, ou catalogue raisonné de livres difficiles à trouver. Par David Clement. Göttingen, 1750-1760." Nine volumes, 4to. Many of the books described in this catalogue, which was carried only to the letter H, have yet to be found; in fact, it is largely conceded that they do not—perhaps never did—exist.

[13] The Giunta edition of Boccaccio, printed at Firenze, 1527, is esteemed the best edition of this famous book. A so-called facsimile was printed at Venice in 1729, but the counterfeit is discovered by the formation of the a, as indicated.

www.ingramcontent.com/pod-product-compliance
Ingram Content Group UK Ltd.
Pitfield, Milton Keynes, MK11 3LW, UK
UKHW040821280325
456847UK00003B/607